The Ninja Shuriken Manual

by Takayuki Kubota

Please note that the publishers and the author of this instructional book are NOT RESPONSIBLE in any manner whatsoever for any injury which may result by reading and/or following the instructions herein.

Also, the possession and/or use of Shuriken or throwing stars for martial arts training or sport may be subject to state and local laws. Please consult your local police or law enforcement agency for the regulations governing your area. We do not imply, condone or encourage that legal regulations be broken. This book is intended for informational purposes only.

For practice purposes and to avoid accidental injuries, it is recommended that hard foam Shuriken be used. Please consult your local police or law enforcement agency for regulations governing foam Shurikens, although they are permissible in most areas. See back page for selection and purchasing information.

Acknowledgement

I would like to express our sincere thanks to those individuals who helped make this book possible: To Master Takayuki Kubota for sharing his extensive knowledge on the subject; to Craig Matsuno for his patient and expert knowledge of photography and design; to Dan Furuya for his careful research into the origins of the Shuriken, and to Grace Higashi, a talented writer, for her story of the "Masakune Ninja".

About the Author

Born in Kumamoto, Japan, in 1934, Master Takayuki Kubota began studying the ancient arts of Karate and Jitsu at the age of four. His insatiable quest for knowledge regarding the martial arts, however, soon carried him throughout Japan, formally and informally studying under masters of many styles, thereby gaining a diverse background which few modern day martial artists could rival.

His teaching career began at the age of fourteen and has flourished since that time. From 1958 to 1964, he instructed United States Military Police and other personnel in self-defense techniques at military bases in Japan. During this time, Master Kubota also served as bodyguard for the United States Ambassador to Japan. Kubota continued his teaching, following his move to the United States in 1964. He has trained numerous criminal justice, military and security personnel from various federal, state and local agencies, including members of the Los Angeles Police Department, Federal Bureau of Investigation and the United States Justice Department.

Primarily known for his Gosoku Ryu Karate and for his training of law enforcement personnel around the world in baton and criminal apprehension techniques, and for the development of his highly effective Kubotan self-defense system, Master Kubota is also an expert in several other martial arts. Besides holding an eighth degree black belt in Aikido Jitsu, a third degree black belt in Judo and a first degree black belt in Kendo, as well as possessing a wealth of knowledge on the ancient weapons and styles of Japan.

He is the president and general instructor of the International Karate Association, Inc., with affiliated schools across the United States and in 22 foreign countries. In addition, he has appeared in many television programs and motion pictures including: *Simon & Simon, The Buffalo Bill Show* and the Sam Peckinpah film, *Killer Elite*, in which he portrayed a Ninja Assassin.

Although busy instructing karate at the IKA World Headquarters in Glendale, California, Master Kubota has found time to write several articles and books on various aspects of police training, karate instruction and personal self-defense. Recently, drawing on his extensive martial arts background, Master Kubota has begun revealing ancient aspects of little known Japanese martial arts and their weapons.

Table of Contents

The Masakune Ninja

Samurai Yoshimura breathes a little easier as the black of night softens with the coming of dawn. Perhaps it's just a rumor after all, he thinks, yet the light is welcome; in the dark too many things are hidden, invisible and evil. The loyal samurai was coming to the end of another night vigil over Lord Tanaka, sleeping in the next room, his form blurred through the thin paper of the shoji. He walks along the veranda overlooking the peaceful garden, then peers into the dark shapes of the forest beyond. Tonight he had been especially alert, having learned that Lord Yone was planning to attack. Evil Yone, he thinks, wreaking havoc throughout Southern Japan by his lust for power, his arrogant amusement with followers who groveled at his feet . . . his greed. Lord Yone had risen through the ranks by sheer force and brutality, using tactics that no true samurai would deem honorable. Yet his devious and systematic elimination of weak and careless lords had gained Yone control over vast and valuable lands. He had gained so much power that now, he had the boldness to go after Lord Tanaka, Yone's most daring move of all. Lord Tanaka is a wise leader and for years has been a fair and honorable Lord to his people. But he is growing old and a likely target for the aggressive Yone. Hatred fills Yoshimura as he thinks about his enemy. He had distrusted him even when they were both young, inexperienced soldiers learning the ways of the samurai, competing to establish themselves as worthy warriors. In the beginning, they had been friends, sharing the hardships of training, but then, Yone has strayed far from the path of honor, growing more and more ruthless as his greed and wealth increased. I look forward to meeting you, Yone, Yoshimura says to himself; I will cut you down with no mercy and with great pleasure. But will you come? Or will you hire the Masakunes to do your filthy work? As he thinks of the fiercest group of mercenaries in Southern Japan, Yoshimura feels his body grow cold and a chill crawl along the back of his neck. Yoshimura had met many opponents during his many years as a warrior, but none unnerved or frightened him more than the confrontation with one of the Masakune Ninjas two years ago. Ah, Sasaki-san, we almost had him captured, didn't we, Yoshimura thinks, vividly recalling that day. We were almost the first to capture a Masakune Ninja, alive! But you acted too rashly in the heat of the battle. If you had not moved so quickly, you might have survived, my friend. Responding to a barely audible noise near their encampment, Yoshimura and Sasaki had gone to investigate, only to find a young Ninja sketching the outline of Lord Yone's camp and noting troop strength. They studied him closely. He was dressed in black, his entire body enveloped with only his eyes visible in the dark of night. An expert artist, he drew the campsite swiftly and with precision, carefully citing measurements, numbers of campfires and men. Suddenly sensing their presence, the Ninja abruptly hurled a small vial of flash powder to the ground, but the samurais, tutored in the tricks of the Ninja, acted instantly, rolling aside, shielding their eyes from the blinding light then, jumping to their feet they drew their swords in a stance, ready for combat. Sasaki attacked first with an ear-splitting kiai, his sword slashed through the air, inflicting a severe wound on the Ninja's arm. Then Yoshimura's sword sliced through the air and two more perfectly placed cuts seemed to make the result of the battle obvious. But then the Ninja threw his Shuriken, hoping yet for a final retreat, hitting Yoshimura. Sasaki dodged the next flying star and moved in to capture the spy. As he approached, his sword ready, raised above his head, the Ninja suddenly drew a bundle from his inner jacket and thrust it in front of his face. Sasaki responded instinctively, striking the bundle with a powerful slash. Yoshimura tried to block the blow, realizing that the Ninja held another explosive, but he was too late. A blinding flash of light blotted out everything, the deafening noise of the blast filled Yoshimura's ears, and the earth shook beneath his feet.

For just a split second, Yoshimura felt surprise, then only blackness as the force of the explosion knocked him unconscious. When he had awakened, Sasaki lay bleeding, his arms torn away, his front a tattered mess of blood and hanging skin. He writhed in agony, clenching his teeth to hold back his cries between curses of his bad luck. Death mercifully released him a short while later. The explosion had totally mutilated the face of the Ninja, erasing all identity, and so, another Masakune Ninja had escaped. The fanatical reputation of the mysterious Masakunes spread through Japan as rapidly as fire raging through the paper and wood structures of the Japanese homes, spurred on by the gust of a dry, unrelenting wind. But theirs was not the only reputation to gain fame across the land. Yoshimura became known for his loyalty, courage and skill in the way of the Samurai code. He had become the trusted and sole protector of

2

Lord Tanaka, proving himself over and over again through many battles and exploits. But as Yoshimura recalled that day, he knew that that night two years ago was not his last encounter with the Masakunes. All night long he had flashing visions of Shurikens ripping through his body, and he imagined that every rustle of leaves or movement in the shadows were the stealthily Ninjas encircling him and Lord Tanaka. An enemy who is silent is difficult to fight, one who is invisible is almost impossible. All he could do was wait, watch and listen - his entire mind, body, and senses focusing on the darkness, becoming one with his surroundings, able to feel a change, an intruder . . . . . .

A bird, the first creature to awaken to meet the dawn, alights on a branch of a tree outside Lord Tanaka's room and begins to peck at the bark. It is startled into flight by a squirrel scrambling up the trunk with its morning meal safely tucked in its cheek. It settles comfortably on the branch once occupied by the bird, nibbling on a morsel. Sensing danger, it stiffens, listens, and sniffs to determine the direction of the enemy. Before it can escape, it is gently scooped up by the leader of the Masakune Ninjas who had moments ago awakened from a trance, hanging motionless in the tree throughout the night. "You must not give away my hiding place little friend",Masakune says to himself, gently stroking the squirrel's head. Feeling the creature tremble, Masakune releases it and watches it scurry away to munch on his breakfast where it will not be so rudely disturbed. Masakune chuckles to himself, always finding delight in the creatures of nature, especially the gentle ones who harm no one. Life is so beautiful when one looks only to nature, Masakune thinks, sighing inwardly as he prepares himself for the glorious coming of morning, the dawn his favorite time of day when all is quiet and slowly awakening, a moment when everything seems to pause, holding its breath in anticipation then slowly releasing it to begin the pulse of life again.

It is the night, however, that is Masakune's world. For in the black oblivion, he is most comfortable, moving with ease, in his element, his five senses intensified, his mind exhilarated, his entire being blending with the ambiguities of the dark. It is them that he performs most of his work, for he is the master of his art, the revered leader of the Ninjas. It has been many years since Masakune had personally gone on a mission. Having perfected the skills of the secret Ninja art and gaining fame as the consummate master above all others, he had been content to pass the last five years training those younger than he in his craft. So his family had been puzzled when he had taken on tonight's request. They had thought he was feeling old, age creeping into his bones early. Yet here he was, going on a mission again and they wondered if it might have something to do with his son. His first born had shown great promise in the art of stealth and Masakune was barely able to hide his pride whenever he looked at him. The son was quick to learn and eager to please his master-father. They were inseparable. Then he had been killed, nearly allowing himself to be captured. An unforgiveable sin for a Ninja. But in the end, he had died bravely, a true Ninja, protecting the secrecy of the clan as well as killing a samurai. His son had begged his permission to enter the samurai encampment to copy the site but Masakune had hesitated, unsure whether his son was adequately prepared. Finally, Masakune's pride overtook him and he consented. The consequences had been fatal. Was he feeling guilt for his decision? No one knew or dared ask, so life continued on as it always

3

does, the boy fading into the recesses of memory, except in the heart of Masakune. That was over two years ago and his heart still ached as strongly as the day he learned of his son's death, not allowing the pain to be released through tears or the comforting from others. The boy was his only son, his only child. He had lost his heart once before when his beloved wife had died in childbirth. But the son had carried the warmth and light of the

mother, keeping her alive for Masakune, and now, they were both gone. I am responsible, my son, for you being killed, Masakune thinks sadly; I let my pride in you cloud my vision and my judgment and I foolishly sent you to your death, though I knew better. I will have no peace until I avenge your death.

Masakune concentrates intensely and, in his mind's eye, visualizes rubbing his hands together over a roaring fire and so his hands become varm. Yet he has not moved for he knows that even the slightest motion might betray him before he is ready. He continues to watch for movement within Lord Tanaka's room. Lord Yone's request had passed through his elaborate network of spies that he had arranged in a pyramid structure - those on the bottom acting as messengers and contacts, the ears of the organization, relaying information to people above, they in turn contacting the next layer until it finally reached the carefully selected and fiercely loyal circle around Masakune who were the only ones privy to all information. Masakune's people were everywhere, infiltrating the castles and fiefs of major and minor daimyos at all levels, working as servants, cooks and maids, living as simple peasants and merchants in almost every major village, the most beautiful of women, courtesans in famous teahouses, who passed on secrets whispered to them by prestigious clients. Some of Masakune's most valuable spies were even trusted advisors to the daimyos. Masakune's empire covered most of Southern Japan, the arms of the organization extending far beyond Masakune's expectations, he the heart and the mind that fueled it all. All of his followers were blood relatives, if not by direct descent then by the sacred oath of blood, swearing allegiance to Masakune regardless of their rank within the structure, sworn to the secrecy of his and their own true identity. The penalty was a cruel death if ever one broke the oath. The eyes of the organization watched the actions of the people within it carefully to monitor traitors and to catch treachery before it blossomed and spread.

The Ninjas, the elite of the organization, were picked from the most promising by master Masakune, who selects the best when they are still toddlers first learning to walk. He senses their potential by his ability to see within the soul and also by looking deeply into their eyes. Those lacking the spark to be ignited into a fire were assigned to lower posts and duties. The Masakune mercenaries consisted of fifty elite men and women who passed the rigors of years of training. This training covered many unusual skills, such as the art of alchemy and the secrets of poisonous plants, breathing exercises which slowed the heartbeat to the brink of death, how to become invisible by becoming a rock, tree or animal, how to prepare special foods for dangerous missions, how to move across pebbles and rooftops without noise, and, or course, the art of throwing the Shuriken. Masakune rarely made errors in his selection of the elite, but a student who failed in his pursuit of the art at any level is invited the release of an honorable death to preserve the secrecy and the perfection vital to the organization. The decision was always painful for Masakune for he hated the useless taking of a life - except in the taking of a life of a samurai. He knew that his clan was reputed to be fanatical killers without motives, no one discovering his true reasons for his becoming the most feared Ninjas.

It is the day that he stopped being the son of a farmer. He closes his eyes as the scenes replay themselves in his mind. The image becomes

clearer, brighter. He is chasing his baby sister around the yard, playing to pass the afternoon away until dinner while his father works nearby, fixing the roof of their home after a heavy rainy season. Suddenly, they hear loud laughter and boisterous voices coming from around the bend of the road that curves by their farm. Masakune and his sister stop playing and wait to see who is coming. Three samurai stagger, drunk, leaning on each other for support, tripping over each other's feet as they walk. Their leader is barely able to sit up on his horse and his head bounces stupidly from side to side with the slow gait. The children begin to giggle but are quickly hushed by their father as he hurries down from the roof and beckons his children to come to him, motioning for them to bow on their knees, their foreheads touching the ground. Masakune watches with fear as they begin to harass his father by pushing and ridiculing him, then ordering him to bring sake, a luxury they know a poor farmer cannot afford. His father begins to apologize, offering tea or water. The samurai become more abusive. The leader climbs off his horse, cursing, and smashes the hilt of his sword into the father's face, reeling around with the force of his own blow and falling to the ground. The others laugh, draw their swords and begin to stab the father, who lies groaning and holding his jaw, blood spilling from a gash in his lip. They order him to get up, striking him each time he tries until, finally, he cannot get up anymore. His clothes, soaked with blood, leave a trail of dirt and blood for a few feet, the length he crawled before collapsing. His mother had run out of the house when the assault began, running to the children to cover their eyes with her body, holding them close to her, crying hysterically, but Masakune continues to watch, paralyzed, unable to take his eyes off his father. Finally, the horror stops. The samurai, still drunk and laughing, pass the children and their mother. They wipe their bloodied swords with a silk sash and wrap it around her neck as a rememberance of their visit. They continue on the road, their laughter lingering long after they have disappeared. Masakune's heart pounds with anger and hate, his whole body and soul trembling. He swears to seek vengeance on all samurai. He swears he will never again feel helpless against their arrogance and power.

From that day, vengeance became his life. He trained every day, first making his body strong, then training his mind in the various martial arts to make himself an invincible weapon. He also studied poisons and explosives as agents of defense, sometimes creating his own. Now, 25 years later, in an ironic twist of fate, he is the pawn in the power game of the samurai. Samurai against samurai, they use him to destroy their enemies,

infiltrate camps and retrieve information, unknowingly fulfilling Masakune's all-consuming with to destroy all men of their class. And each time he
received a request, he silently thanked them for their selfishness and
foolish games.

And then, five years ago, he had had enough of killing. He felt that his
father's death had been avenged and the fire of hatred left his soul. Thus,

he taught for several years and let the younger ones do the killing. Until the death of his son. It was then that the smoldering ashes of his hate burst into flames once again. But three years had passed since he'd gone on a mission and by now, he had lost much of his skill. His hand was not as sure, it trembled slightly so that he could not throw a Shuriken with the same precise accuracy as before. At the peak of his skill, with a slight, quick snap of his wrist, the star would fly through the air, tear through the shoji and hit a target with deadly accuracy on the other side, then be quickly followed by a second star hurtling along the same deadly path. So it shall be again, he thought to himself when his son died, I was master once. I will be master again

So, for two long years, Masakune practiced as he had before. Again and again, he threw the Shuriken, trying just one at first, until his aim was perfect. Then he threw two in quick succession, then three, then four and so on until, at last, he was ready. When Lord Yone's request came, he knew that the mission was his alone. His son's death had gone too long un-avenged, the killer had lived much longer than he should have, shaming the Ninja for being unable to more quickly show honor to his only son.

Now, his target was within reach. His whole body surged with such tre-mendous vibrating energy that it was almost possible to see rays ema-nating from his being. His mind became alert with a sharpness that could sense an eyelash fall. The enemy was so close that he felt the filling urge leap into his fingertips, and the force of the sensation touched the Shu-riken in his sleeves, making them charged and trembling.

Makakune pulls out a Shuriken from his sleeve, rotating it carefully be-tween his fingers to release the tension in his wrist and to loosen and warm the fingers joints, avoiding the sharp points dipped in poison. The cold metal warms quickly in his hands. He edges himself along the branch and eases himself into a sitting position, wrapping his legs around it for bal-ance, With his other hand, he reaches into his sleeve and pulls out a second Shuriken. His eyes narrow as he concentrates on Lord Tanaka, calculating and measuring the distance. He is ready.

A maid gracefully walks up the veranda, her tabi brushing whispered strokes against the wooden floor as she carries a lacquered tray with hot tea. Lord Tanaka enjoys "ocha" in the early morning immediately upon awakening to end a night of restful sleep and to begin a new day. She kneels outside his room and places the tray tenderly down for she is fond of the old Lord. With both hands she slides the shoji open and greets the just-arising Lord with a good morning and hopes that his sleep was undisturbed and refreshing. Still seated, she bows, turns and reaches for her tray. Suddenly, a Shuriken zings by her, a fraction of an inch from her face, brushing the stray hair upon her forehead. She screams as the Shuriken strikes Lord Tanaka in the chest, an expression of surprise on his face. He grabs his chest, his face twists and contorts as the pain sears through his body. A strangled moan escapes his throat and he falls for-ward into the folds of the futon.

Like a dream, a nightmare, his consciousness detached from his body, Yoshimura watches the Shuriken spin through the rice paper and plunge into Lord Tanaka's body. Ninja, his mind alerts, then explodes as his body awakens into action. He ducks instinctively, scuttling across the floor like a crab to avoid the next Shuriken he knows is aimed at him. He speaks harshly to the maid, who cowers trembling, her hands and arms covering her head, telling her to run. Her body responds to his command.

8

She runs into the room to escape but trips over Lord Tanaka's body. Without thinking, Yoshimura rushes toward her, grabs her, then pushes her through the inner door and lunges as a second Shuriken barely misses him. His ears fill with the sound of his own panting, fear thumping in his eardrums, his mouth dry, his chest rising and falling rapidly, his sword gripped in his hand so tightly that his knuckles are white. Be calm, he thinks to himself, in a vain attempt to stop the panic rising in his throat. Play *your* battle, not *his*, make him come to you; otherwise you are defeated. From the sky Masakune drops to the veranda. For a moment they stare at each other, the Ninja crouching, his arm cocked over his head, the Shuriken catching the glint of the sun, and Yoshimura also ready to pounce like a tiger, each offering a silent challenge, daring the other to move first. Yoshimura springs to his feet, then rushes for Masakune, his sword slashing quickly back and forth in the air in an attempt to block the trajectory of a poisonous star. Masakune remains motionless, then throws the star just as the point of the sword slashes inches from his face, then rolls to the side as Yoshimura crumples and pitches forward from the momentum of his attack, his hand clutching his shoulder where the Shuriken has pierced his flesh, his sword tumbling to the floor as his arm locks, paralyzed by the poison. He stumbles at the Ninja's feet when Masakune thrusts a second star into his heart. He reaches for the dagger in his belt in a last atempt to avenge his lord, but begins to feel disoriented as the poison rapidly spreads through his body. He sways to his feet, then stumbles, feebly slashing at Masakune. The Ninja master catches him as he falls, gently laying him down on the tatami floor as death quickly overtakes Yoshimura, the poison engulfing his body entirely. The tears finally fall as Masakune watches the samurai leave this life. May you return as a Masakune, he thinks, for he had seen the fire burning within Yoshimura brighter then any other samurai he had encountered. For a moment his hatred subsides; an honorable samurai? He questions, then scoffs at the thought. You were born into the wrong class. May you return as one of us. Masakune places a bundle underneath Yoshimura's head and runs out into the forest as the alarm spreads thoughout the camp. He pauses briefly to watch Lord Tanaka's room explode violently and brilliantly, fire erupting from the shatter paper and wood. Smoke billows to the sky, Masakune turns and continues his journey silently, swiftly home, the master Ninja once again.

History of the Shuriken

Most scholars agree that the earliest Shuriken or throwing stars appeared sometime during the latter half of the 14th century. However, the first mention of the Shuriken, in ancient documents related to martial arts in Japan, appears around the 15th century during the Segoku Jidai or "Age of Civil Wars" in Japan when many feudal lords were vying for power and territorial control.

The exact origin of the Shuriken is unknown but there are three important currents which contributed to its development. Warfare during the Sengoku Jidai was marked by an increase in hand-to-hand combat known as *gusoku*, which was the forerunner of many jujitsu schools. Because most of the combatants wore some sort of protective armour on the battlefield, a very short dirk or dagger became popular to thrust in between the armour plates when the opponent was thrown to the ground or held in a joint-lock technique. This dirk was much shorter and thicker than the *tanto* or traditional dagger of the period, approximately 11 to 14 inches long. It was approximately 7 to 9 inches long and very thick, and was known as a *yoroi dooshi* or armour piercer. Some were double-edged to cut both ways in close combat and were known as *moroha zukuri*. Because of the special nature and techniques involved with this type of dirk, they were classified under *tanto-uchi* (striking with a dagger) or simply *uchimono* (striking techniques). Many *atemiwaza* or striking techniques used in jujitsu today were originally techniques designed to strike the body with this type of weapon instead of a fist. This weapon was distinct from the sword and dagger worn by the warriors. It was often carried on the opposite or right side of the belt as opposed to the left sword side, as a result, called *me-dasashi* (right-side wearing). In *uchimono* techniques, the dirks were often thrown at the opponents at close range.

Shuriken literally means "held or concealed in the hand", which indicates its original usage as a type of dagger. Gradually, masters began to develop their own forms of this weapon, more suitable or effective to their personal needs in striking or throwing. Legend has it that during this time, many Ninja clans adopted the Shuriken for their own uses and developed them as a highly effective throwing weapon.

The second influence on the Shuriken was the *uchine*, which appeared in the 17th century. It was an obscure weapon resembling a shortened arrow with a thick shaft and point, much like a short spearhead. It is believed that they were originally thrown by hand from horseback against foot soldiers. Examples found today are of recent construction made for commoners who were not permitted to carry long swords.

A third theory is that the Shuriken was introduced from China. The exact dates are unknown, but it was probably sometime during the 17th century when mention was first made of it. This weapon was known as the *byo*

10

(Chinese: biao), which literally means "the point of a sword or spear". This was introduced in a secret throwing technique known as *sanfuka jitsu* or the three-in-one technique. Three byo were thrown at one time, with one aimed at the target and two to distract the opponent. (The Ninja utilized a similar technique with two straight Shuriken.)

The Shuriken is popularly known as the weapon of the Ninja and they did much to refine them and to improve throwing techniques, however, it was also used, to some degree, by martial artists and commoners alike because it was easily concealed and effective at close range.

There were approximately thirty different public schools of Shuriken techniques, of which only a few exist today. Some schools still in existence are the Ikeda, Araki, Yagyu, Katori Shinto, Tsukawa and Shirai. Closed or "secret" schools of the art still exist, but are generally small and little is known of their teachings.

There are three major types of Shuriken. The first is the *bo-shuriken* or straight shaft, which is the oldest and most common form. Known for its penetrating ability and use as a hand-held weapon, this type of Shuriken was difficult to master and therefore did not gain popular acceptance as a throwing weapon. It was integrated into the arsenal of certain Ninja groups who favored this type of Shuriken for its penetrating power. Extensive training in power throwing techniques combined with a thorough understanding of trajectory and distance allowed them to deliver lethal strikes to an opponent's throat, heart or main artery.

The *jujiken* or cross-shaped Shuriken was originally a crudely developed throwing star primarily used to distract an opponent, although some Ninja refined this type of Shuriken into a very effective (offensive) weapon.

Finally, the most sophisticated and popular type were the *kuruma-ken* or wheel-shaped Shuriken. They were easily concealed and could be thrown in rapid succession. Most Shuriken found today fall into this type. They were relatively accurate even when thrown long distances.

Most Ninja adopt all three types and refine their techniques to utilize the strengths of each type.

Types of Shuriken

A small sampling of the thousands of variations of Shuriken. There are three basic types of Shuriken: The *bo-shuriken* or straight shaft Shuriken, which is the oldest form; the *jujiken* or cross-shaped Shuriken and the *kuruma-ken* or wheel-shaped Shuriken. Most Shuriken found today fall into the last category, with some being a combination of the *jujiken* and the *kuruma-ken.*

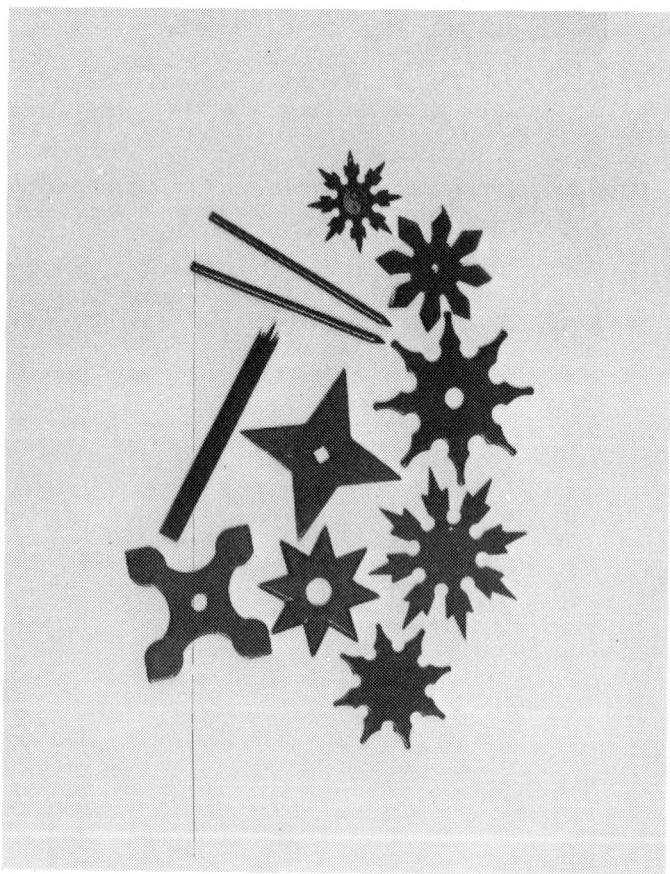

STAR SHURIKEN

Types of Throws

Used when maximum power and accuracy is desired. This is the easiest throw to master. The key is proper timing in the release and good follow thru (fingers should end up pointing at the target).

This throw is used when an element of surprise is desired. Thrown from a seemingly non-offensive stance. Although minimal power can be generated, accuracy can be achieved with extensive practice. No follow thru is required but proper timing of the release is essential

Used when maximum power is desired. Utilizes the torque of the hips, shoulder and elbow by crossing the body from approximately the ear to the waist. Extensive practice is essential to develop the proper timing for the release.

Used primarily to throw around trees, walls, etc. This throw offers maximum power with minimal exposure of the body to attack by an opponent. Thrown from the ear to the waist. Proper timing of the release and follow thru is essential for accuracy.

★ Angular throws can be adapted to any of the above.

NOTE: All instruction assumes right-handed thrower. Reverse all instruction for left hand. You should practice with both hands to the point where you can accurately hit the target with either hand.

Types of Grips

STANDARD OR BASIC GRIP/
WITH STRAIGHT INDEX FINGER

This is the basic beginning grip for throwing star training. The star is held firmly between the thumb and index finger. Begin by making a fist with the index finger pointing forward. Grasp the star in a vertical position (tips pointing up and down) between the index finger and the thumb. On release, the index finger remains stationary, while the thumb is relaxed, releasing the star. You should finish with your index finger pointing toward the target. Begin practice with the overhead throw, then progress to the sidearm throw. This grip may also be used to gain a better hold on larger stars.

Side View

Front View

Back View

STANDARD OR BASIC GRIP

This is a variation of the "Standard or Basic Grip with Straight Index Finger". In this grip the star is similarly pinched between the thumb and the index finger, however the index finger is bent along with the other fingers to form a fist. This grip only controls the release, while speed, power and rotation are controlled by the wrist, hips and arm. This grip is best suited for either sidearm throw or the overhead throw.

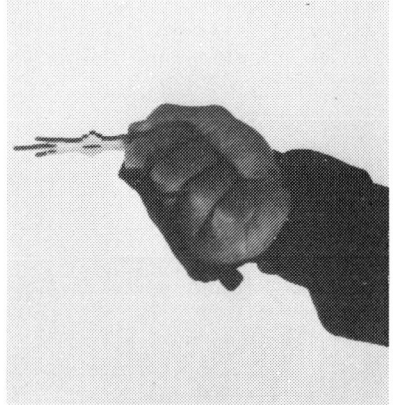

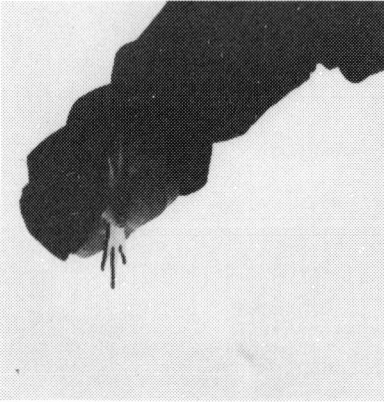

STANDARD OR BASIC GRIP (FOR SMALL STARS)

This variation of the "Standard or Basic Grip" utilizes the index finger as a cradle to hold small stars. Using a similar fist grip with the index finger slightly bent, press the thumb over approximately ⅓ of the star for maximum control and power. For obvious reasons, smaller stars have limited penetration power.

This grip is ideal for close range training or target practice. A flick of the wrist should give sufficient velocity to stick into most targets and consistent accuracy can be attained with practice.

KNUCKLE GRIP

This is a slightly more advanced Shuriken grip. The star is held between the index and middle knuckle. The thumb presses down on the index finger to give additional grip control. The remaining fingers are held in a fist position.

The Knuckle Grip is primarily used to throw stars with the backhand style, utilizing maximum power from the arm and elbow. Initially practice the overhead throw, as you must first master the release. When the grip release is mastered, progress to the sidearm and underhand throws. This is a quick snapping release. The arm should only travel a short distance, combined with a quick snap of the wrist.

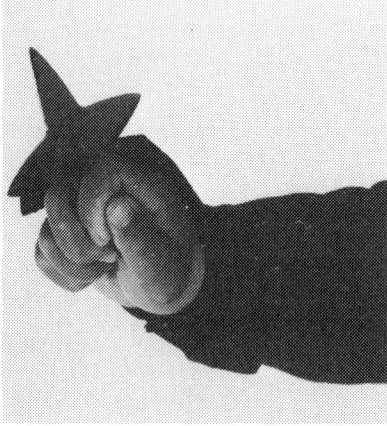

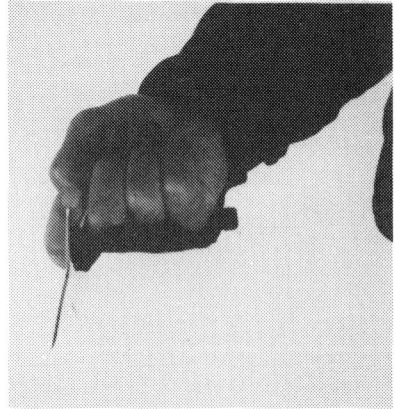

WRIST-SNAPPING GRIP

Primarily used with small Shuriken, this grip develops the needed velocity by snapping the wrist. Hold the star between the index and middle finger with the thumb tucked in. All fingers should be straight with no gaps between the individual fingers.

This is not a power grip as neither the hips, lower body or the shoulders are used. Extensive practice is required to develop a smooth, accurate release. This is also a very versatile grip, as stars can be thrown at a fairly rapid rate and from any angle.

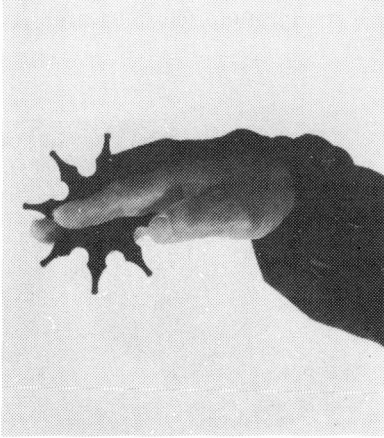

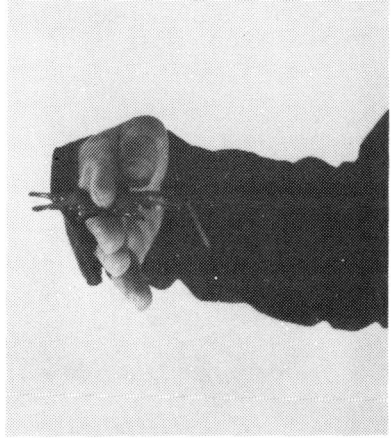

POWER GRIP

As the name implies, this grip is used when maximum penetrating power is desired. Primarily used with the 4 point stars, the Power Grip utilizes the elbow joint in combination with the snapping of the wrist to achieve maximum power. Grasp the star loosely in the palm of the hand. The index finger is straight and should end up, after release, pointing at the target. The thumb is used merely to guide the star on a smooth release. The grip and subsequent release is controlled by the last three fingers, which open upon release.

This is a deceptive grip, which hides a good portion of the star from view. The Ninja found this to be a very versatile grip, from which they could conceal a star at their side to be thrown at an opponent without warning or to be used as a close-in fighting weapon.

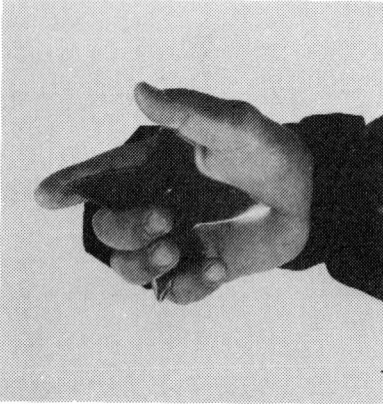

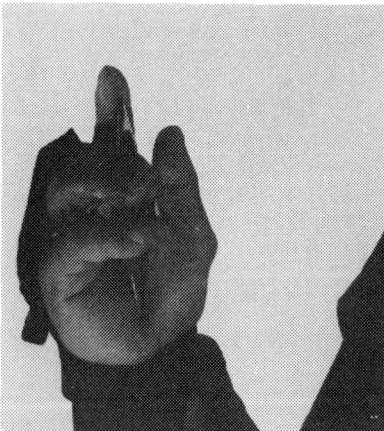

ANGULAR THROWING GRIP

The Angular Throwing Grip is similar to the "Standard or Basic Grip", except the wrist and arm are twisted slightly to give the star a 45° angle trajectory upon release. Tremendous power can be generated with practice, but care must be taken to develop a controlled release.

This grip is best suited for the sidearm throw and primarily used with large stars for maximum power and penetration.

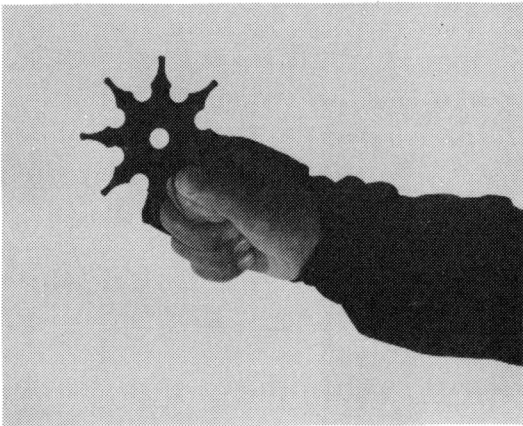

POWER GRIP II

This grip is very similar to "Power Grip I" but is used primarily with *Kuruma-ken* type of stars (stars with multiple points). Place the star in the palm of the hand. Again the thumb acts as a guide, as does the index finger, which is straight. The last two fingers control release along with the middle finger.

This is a very difficult grip to master because the fingers must open in sequence for a smooth release. A snapping of the wrist just prior to release gives rotation to the star. Follow thru should end with the index and middle fingers pointing toward the target.

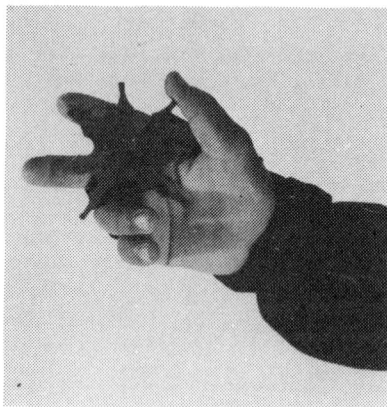

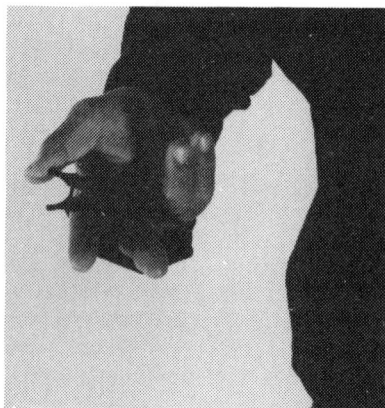

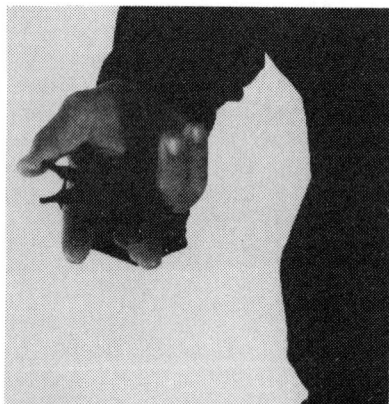

DOUBLE GRIP

This is the final throwing grip and the most difficult to master. Each single hand grip should be practiced with each hand before attempting to throw with both hands simultaneously. Athough any grip can be utilized. this is primarily for overhead throws. This grip was used by Ninja against a single opponent to insure a direct hit or against two opponents. They can be thrown simultaneously or in succession.

Stances & Throwing Techniques

As in all martial arts styles, a variety of stances are utilized to provide a solid foundation for different techniques. The same holds true for Shuriken throwing. The basic stances will be discussed in the following pages. Once these are mastered, a person can create the variations necessary for his/her particular needs.

It should be noted that the major purpose of each stance is to give a person a solid foundation from which they can throw Shuriken, given the terrain and obstacles which may exist.

HORSE STANCE *KIBA DACHI*

The Horse Stance is the fundamental training stance for Shuriken training. The advantages include: a firm foundation from which a person can concentrate on developing proper throwing and follow thru techniques, and disciplined leg training.

Facing the target, place the feet parallel to each other approximately 1½ shoulder width apart. Bend the knees slightly forward, keeping the back straight and the shoulders squared forward. Weight should be evenly distributed on both legs. Hold the star in line with the target. The elbow should be bent and the wrist cocked back. (You should be able to sight down the star to the target.)

Relax, exhale, inhale as you cock back the arm slightly behind the head. Exhale while snapping the arm forward, snapping the wrist at the last second prior to release of the star. Hand should end up pointing at the target.

Front View

Side View

Sighting the target

Cocking the star behind the head

Release and follow thru

26

FRONT STANCE WITH FRONT HAND THROW
ZENKUTSU DACHI

This is the strongest throwing stance for a reverse sidearm throw and is a favorite choice when maximum penetration is desired.

The feet are positioned approximately 1½ shoulder width apart with the rear toes pointed out and the front toes pointed forward. Knees bent, back straight or leaning slightly forward. 75% of the weight should be on the front leg with 25% on the back.

For the reverse sidearm throw from the ready position, exhale, cock star back to a position behind the ear, shifting weight back to 65% on the front leg and 35% on the rear leg, inhaling. Whip arm forward to the original weight distribution while exhaling. Snap wrist just prior to release and follow thru pointing at an imaginary point to the right of the target.

It is essential that you practice the release and follow thru before introducing your full power to maintain control and to develop accuracy. Be careful no to overshift your weight to the front leg.

The ready position

Cocking the star behind the ear

Releasing the star

Follow thru

FRONT STANCE WITH REVERSE HAND THROW
ZENKUTSU DACHI GYAKU NAGE

This is the strongest throwing stance for an overhead throw. It is fairly easy to master and used for accuracy in target training or competition. This stance is identical to the "Front Stance with Front Hand Throw" except for the sighting, cocking and follow thru.

Sight the target in line with the star in a vertical position, cock star back behind the head shifting your weight in the process and inhaling. Whip arm forward with locked wrist, pivoting forward to the original weight distribution while exhaling. Snap wrist just prior to release. Follow thru, pointing at the target.

Sighting the target

Pulling arm back in line of sight with target

Cocking the star behind the ear

Rapid thrust to target, release and follow thru.

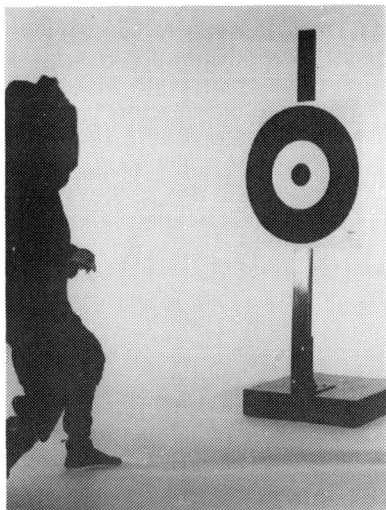
In target practice, cocking the star back.

Rapid thrust to target and release.

Follow thru.

BACK STANCE *KOKUTSU DACHI*

Another very powerful stance for the overhead throw. Excellent for accuracy in target training or competition. The right leg should be back approximately 1 ½ shoulder width, toes perpendicular to the shoulders. Left leg forward, toes pointing forward. Back straight, shoulders squared to the front, knees slightly bent with weight approximately 60% on the back leg and 40% on the front leg.

Sight target, relax and exhale. Cock arm back, tensing slightly, and inhaling. Shift weight smoothly to 65% - 70% on the back leg and 30% - 35% on the front leg. Shoulders twisted to 45° angle. Bring arm forward rapidly shifting weight to 50% on the front leg and 50% on the back leg, exhaling as you release. Use the torque of the hips to gain power.

Sighting the target

Pulling back to cock position, Front View

Side View

Rapid thrust to target, release and follow thru

STANCE *REI DACHI*

Used by the Ninja when throwing Shuriken from behind tall brush or from a hidden position. Requires a minimal amount of body movement which would otherwise give their position away.

Left leg back approximately ¾ shoulder width, toes pointing forward, right leg forward. Both knees slightly bent, back bent forward, shoulders square to the front.

This is primarily a reverse sidearm throwing stance. The power is derived from a quick snapping motion utilizing the shoulder, elbow and wrist.

Star is held at chest level with the wrist locked in a bent position. Cock star back 6" to 8", quickly snap forward, breaking the wrist at the final moment prior to release.

⅔ View, ready position

Rapid-thrust to target, just prior to release

Follow thru

CAT STANCE *NEKO ASHI DACHI*

Used extensively by Ninja because it allowed them to accurately deliver their Shuriken to several angles from a confined position. Left leg back approximately ¾ shoulder width, foot pointed forward or slightly out. Right leg forward on the ball of the foot. 85% of the weight on the left leg, 15% of the weight on the ball of the right foot. Knees bent, back straight, shoulders square to the front.

Cock star back to ear level, inhaling. Do not shift weight during cocking motion. Release in a rapid whipping motion with a breaking of the wrist at the final second. Follow thru with fingers pointing at the target.

The Cat Stance is primarily for the overhead and the reverse sidearm throws. On rare occasions the underhand throw may be used. As this stance is designed for use in very confined areas, little or no body movement should be used.

Front View of ready position

Side View

Thrusting forward to target

Follow thru, holding body position until star hits

ONE LEG STANCE *IPPON DACHI*

Used by Ninja when forced to throw accurately while standing on a rock, or other confined place. Stand on left leg with knee bent, right leg acts as a shock absorbing mechanism.

Hold star at chest level, sight target, exhale. Cock arm back to opposite shoulder (not to the neck, as this would twist the body too much causing instability), and inhale. Use the left arm for balance. Whip arm forward releasing star and follow thru pointing at the target, exhaling. The elbow and wrist should be parallel to the ground.

Primarily used with the reverse sidearm throw because the power is generated in the torquing of the hips.

Training Hint: This is a very difficult stance to master. In the beginning, don't worry about accuracy and power. Concentrate on balance and proper form.

⅔ View of sighting target

Front View of ready position

Side View

Follow thru, holding position

KNEELING STANCE *HIZA DACHI*

An offensive stance used by the Ninja when they stalked an opponent (See "Practical Training"). This stance could be used to throw forward or to either side without exposing themselves. Kneel on right leg, left leg up, back straight.

Sight target holding the star at eye level, exhale. Cock back to behind the ear for maximum power, inhaling, release, breaking wrist at the last second, while exhaling.

This stance is primarily for the overhead or sidearm throws. All power is developed from the upper body only, especially the arm and wrist.

Sighting the target

Cocking the star behind the head

⅔ View of release position

Side View

SEATED STANCE *SUWARI DACHI*

This is not a traditional offensive stance but rather a response to an attack. The Ninja used this as a counter to a high attack by an opponent with a sword, spear, etc. Also used as a retreating response to slow the opponent's pursuit.

The left leg is bent and tucked under the body, while the right leg acts as a front support. 20% of the weight is on the left hand, 60% of the weight is on the left leg and 20% on the right leg. The body is pointed toward the target while the torso is at a 45° angle.

Line up star with the target at eye level. Cock back (shoulder should almost hit the chin), inhaling. Release in an upward trajectory, exhaling. The power is generated from the arm, wrist and shoulder only. This is a quick throw, designed to slow or distract an opponent; it is not a power throw.

Used with the overhead or reverse sidearm throws only.

Training Hint: Because this is a response to an attack by an opponent rather than a stationary throwing stance, practice in two parts. Initially, develop your accuracy and power from the seated position, then practice dropping from a standing position to the *Suwari Dachi* position. Finally put both parts together and practice until this becomes a rapid, accurate movement.

Sighting the target at eye level

Thrust forward, just prior to release

Follow thru, holding position

Side View

Side View of follow thru, note body angle is held

FRONT-SEATED STANCE *MAE SUWARI DACHI*

Used by the Ninja when waiting for or stalking an opponent. The Ninja would find a well-camouflaged area where he was hidden from view. The left leg is crossed and tucked tight under the body. The right leg is pointed toward the target.

Sight target at eye level. Cock Shuriken back to the ear, inhaling. Rapidly whip forward, exhaling. Follow thru by pointing at the target.

Designed for the overhead throw only. Power is generated from the arm, as excess movement would give away a person's hidden position.

Front View, sighting the target

Side View

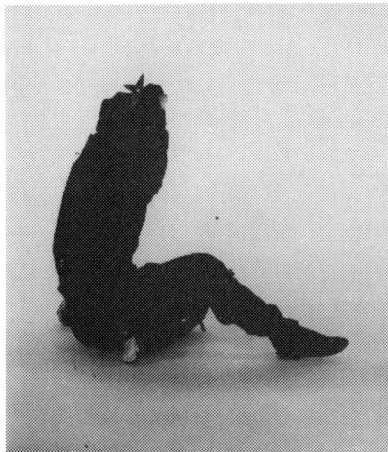

Side View, cocking the star

Rapid thrust to target

Follow thru

THE STRAIGHT SHURIKEN

The straight of *bo shuriken* were the earliest recorded type of throwing star, ranging in length from 4 to 8 inches with one or two pointed ends. Often of tubular steel or iron, many were flat and very similiar to modern day throwing knives. They were used for throwing or as a close combat, hand-held weapon.

The Ninja favored this type of Shuriken to deliver poisons at close range. Two types of throws were used with the straight Shuriken. The non-rotational or direct throw was most often used for close range situations. It had very little penetrating power and was used to deliver poisons or to distract an opponent; the rotational throw was used for middle to long range conditions. When mastered, this was a very powerful, penetrating throw which could cause great damage if accurately delivered.

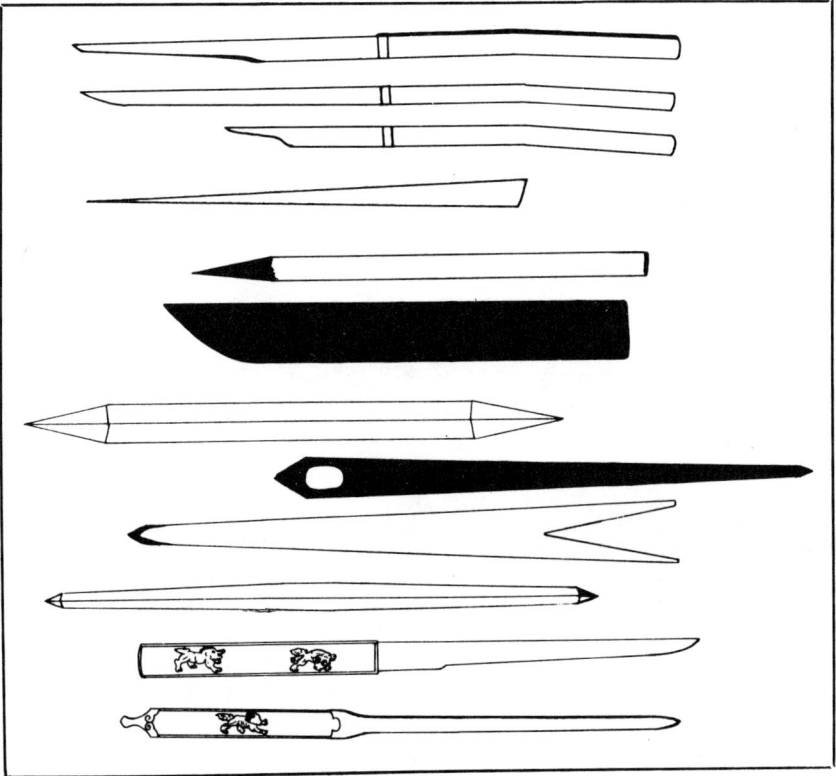

A variety of Straight Shuriken

Types of Trajectory for Straight Shuriken

Rotational.
For middle to long distance (15 to 25 feet)

Non-Rotational.
For short to middle distance throwing (5 to 15 feet)

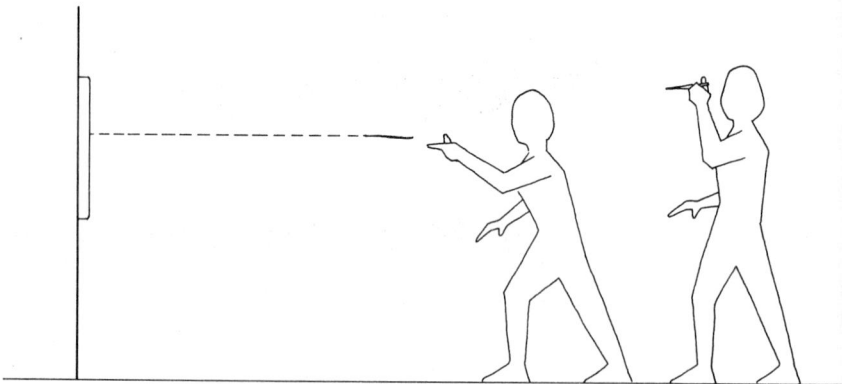

Types of Grips

ROTATIONAL GRIP

Standard or Basic Grip

Make a fist, then grip the Shuriken between the thumb and index finger approximately 1" from the blunt end. This is the standard grip for rotational trajectory throwing and is used with the sidearm or overhead throws. A key to effective throwing is to develop an accurate feel for distance, rotation and speed of the Shuriken.

Maximum range: 25 feet.

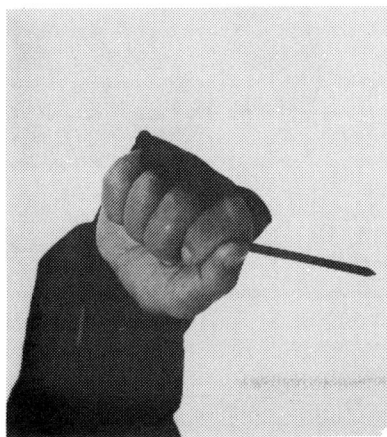

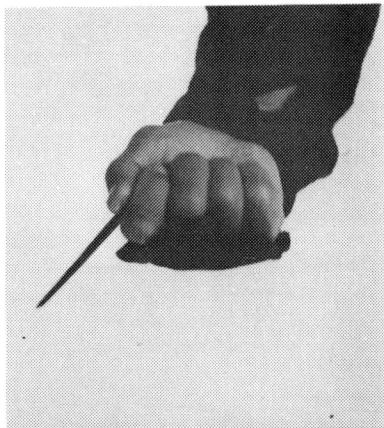

Two-Finger Grip

Hold the Shuriken between the index and middle finger with the remaining three fingers held in a loose fist or resting against the palm. This is a difficult grip, primarily used for overhead throws.
Maximum range: 15 to 20 feet.

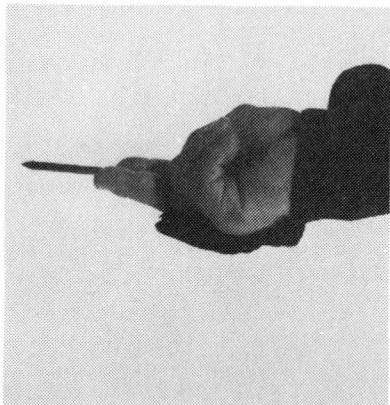

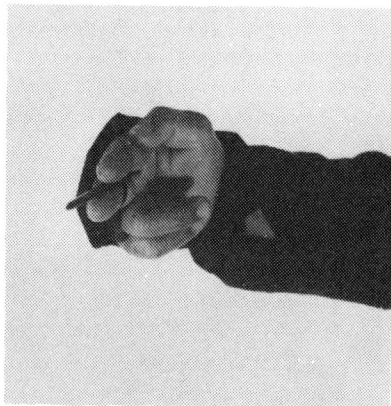

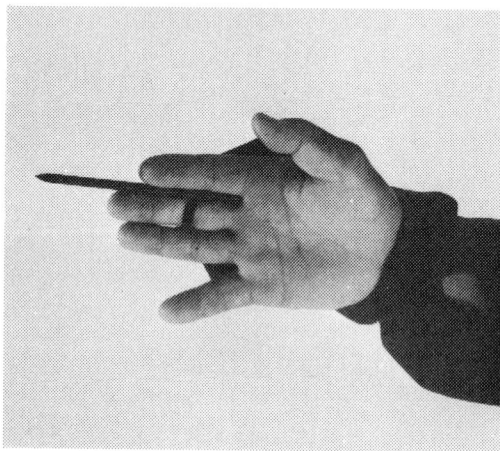

NON-ROTATIONAL GRIP

Straight Grip
The Shuriken is held in the palm of the hand, between the thumb and the index finger. The index finger should be straight while the remaining fingers form a fist. This is a very difficult grip to master, as smooth release is absolutely essential. For overhead or underhand throws.
Maximum range: 15 feet.

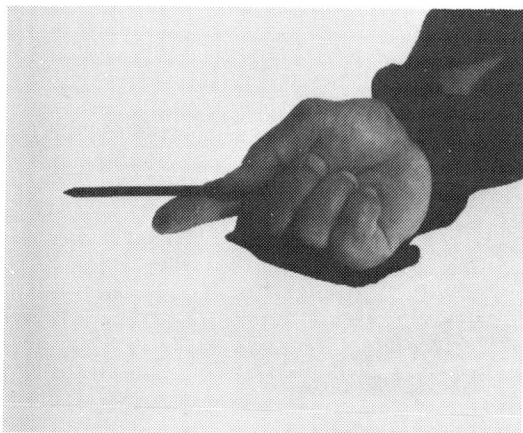

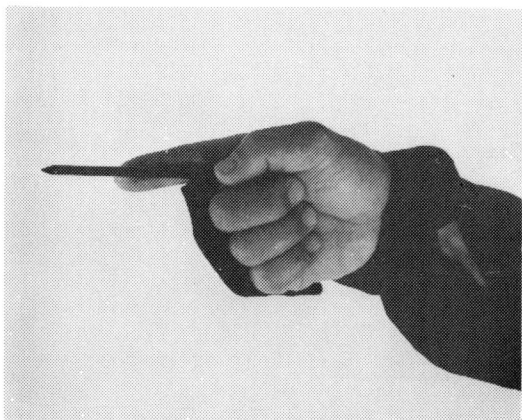

Spear Grip

Hold the Shuriken between the thumb and index finger approximately 2" from the blunt end. The remaining fingers should be held in a loose fist. This is a short distance grip which derives power from a quick snapping of the wrist. Used by Ninja to deliver poison or cause a distraction from very close range, usually from a well-hidden position. Maximum range: 10 feet.

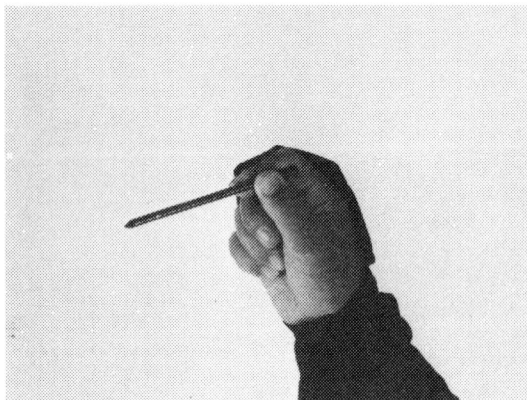

Double Throwing Grip

Grip two straight Shuriken between the thumb and index finger with the tips pointing at a 30° angle from each other. This grip is used for two distinct purposes: Either to provide a "shotgun" effect when thrown one after the other or to aim one at the target while the other is used to distract the opponent. This rotational throw is most effective using the overhead or sidearm trajectory.

Maximum range: 15 feet.

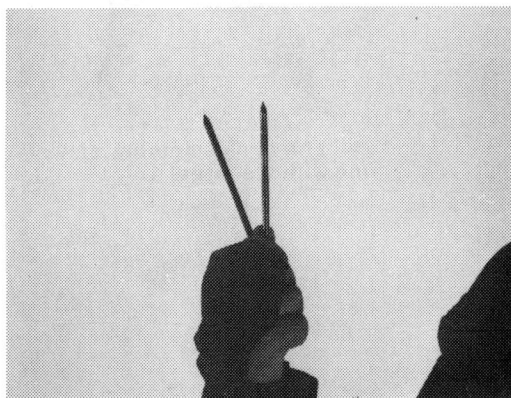

STANCES & THROWING TECHNIQUES

The same stances used for the wheel-shaped *kuruma-ken* type of throwing stars are also used for the Straight Shuriken.

Training Hints: In the beginning, concentrate on the throwing form only, utilizing the same power and speed each time you throw. For rotational throws, don't worry if your Shuriken are not penetrating or sticking to the targets.

Once you have developed a smooth release and good throwing form, begin to adjust your distance from the target until you can consistently penetrate it.

Next, move closer and repeat. Eventually you will be able to adjust your power and speed to strike a target consistently at any distance.

Take sight of the target.

Pull arm back smoothly, staying in line with the target.

Cock to ear level, inhaling, then . . .

Whip arm forward, releasing Shuriken along sight line while exhaling.

Ninja Shuriken Training

Once the basics of the Shuriken were developed, the Ninja would embark in practical training for the student. It was not only important that they know the dynamics of the throwing stars but they must also be equipped with the knowledge and experience of how to deliver the Shuriken from behind trees, bushes, walls, etc. This information may one day save the Ninja's life by allowing him to correctly choose the proper stance and throwing technique for any given location and situation.

KNEELING STANCE *HIZA DACHI*

The Kneeling Stance *Hiza Dachi* is ideally suited for training behind small bushes, walls or trees. The target can be carefully monitored from a hidden position until the right moment arises.

Stalking the target from a hidden position.

Preparing to deliver a Shuriken by sighting the target.

Cocking the Shuriken.

Delivering the Shuriken with proper follow thru.

Note: For practical indoor practice a potted plant as shown above can be used to simulate outdoor combat conditions.

FRONT STANCE *ZENKUTSU DACHI*

The Front Stance with a sidearm throw is ideal for throwing around a tree or wall, while keeping the majority of the body hidden.

Sight the target thru the limbs of the tree.

Cock the star back and whip arm around the obstacle.

Release the star, keeping the majority of the body hidden behind the tree.

KNEELING STANCE II *HIZA DACHI II*

This adaptation of the Kneeling Stance has the practitioner kneeling on both knees. Because of the limited mobility it offered the thrower, this stance was used primarily when an accurate, planned strike was required. Training included kneeling in this position for hours, motionless, until signaled, then a quick and accurate strike was delivered.

Using a box, chair or low table (approximately 3' tall), sight the target and cock back.

Rapidly thrust the arm with a whipping motion, using power from the upper body.

Follow thru, using the other arm to stay stabilized.

For a reverse sidearm throw from the Kneeling Stance, sight the target with the throwing arm partially cocked.

Cock back.

Rapidly whip arm forward, releasing the star.

51

The Sport of Shuriken Throwing

TARGET TRAINING

The Target

A paper, round "bull's eye" target (approximately 12" diameter) is affixed to a 1" thick, soft pine board. (This can be purchased from any lumber or home improvement store or targets can be obtained from a martial arts store or an archery equipment store.)

Attach a picture frame hanger to the back of the target board. Next, in a 2" X 4" X 8' post, hammer hanging nails in at 5 foot and 8 foot intervals. Locate a suitable outdoor/indoor location, allowing at least 2 to 3 feet of space between the target and the back wall or fence. Sink the 2" X 4" X 8' post firmly into the ground (approximately 2' deep). It's a good idea to put a backdrop tarp or old blanket behind the target to prevent stray Shuriken from striking the wall. Hang it high enough to catch stray stars (at least 7' high).

Alternate: You can also use a dart board or throwing star target board. Be sure to secure it in place and use a backdrop to catch stray stars.

Caution: **Be sure that people or pets stay well clear of the target area.**

Tournament Throwing
(Target Point Values)

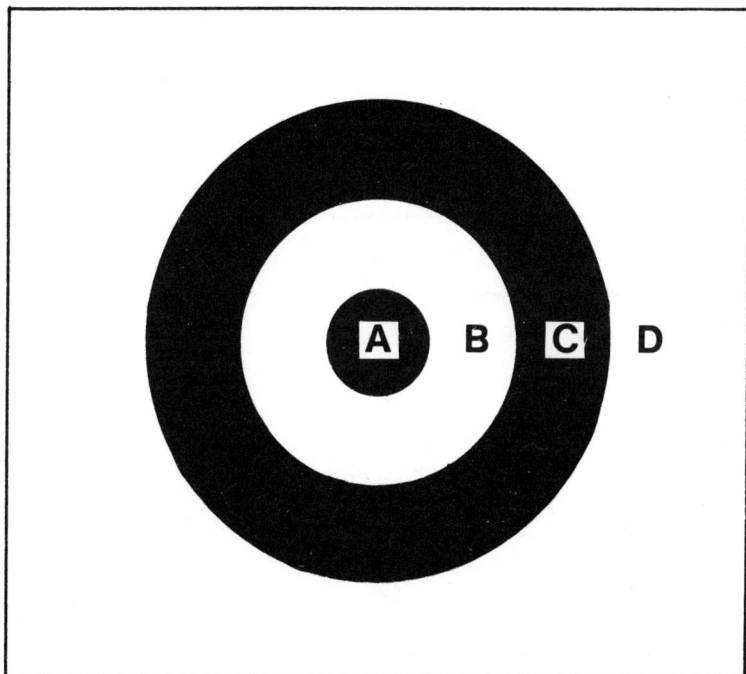

	A	B	C	D
8'	3	1	½	0
10'	10	4	2	0
15'	25	10	5	1
25'	70	30	15	2
30'	100	50	25	5

POINTS SCORED

Tournament Throwing (Floor Layout)

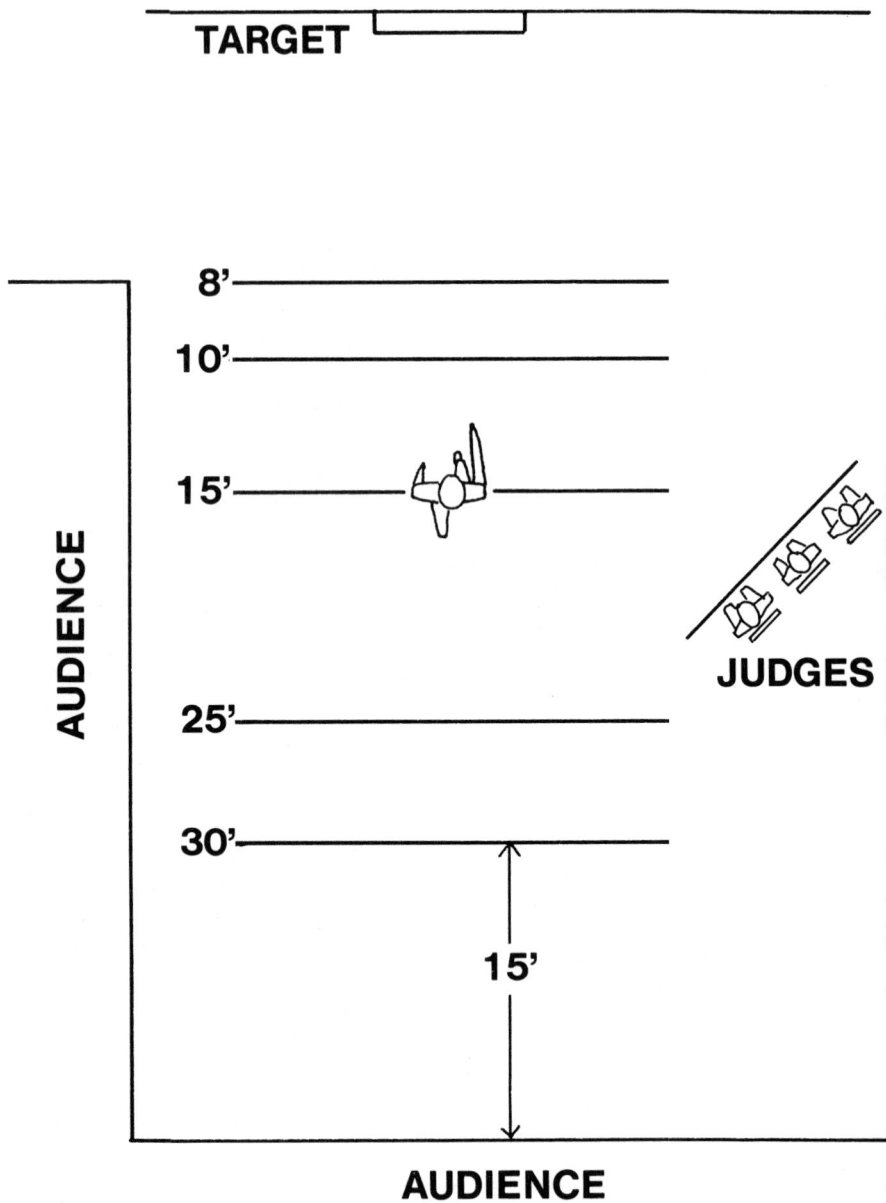

TARGET

8'

10'

15'

AUDIENCE

JUDGES

25'

30'

15'

AUDIENCE

SHURIKEN THROWING COMPETITION (FORMAL)

All regular competition rules apply with the following exceptions and additions:

1. Each person is required to use the standard type of Shuriken established for the competition. No exceptions.
2. Formal competion is to 500 points instead of 100 points.
3. Each contestant starts with 5 standard Shuriken.
4. Any star which fails to hit the target is eliminated from the arsenal of that contestant. (Example: If a contestant misses the target with 3 of his stars, he can continue the competition with his remaining 2!) Stars which hit the target and fall off are not eliminated.
5. If your star knocks an opponents star from the target, that person receives no points and you receive his points for that particular star. (Full points if your star sticks, half the points if your star does not.)
6. Contestants must use 8 of the 10 stances (*Kiba Dachi, Zenkutsu Dachi, Zenkutsu Dachi Gyaku Nage, Kokutsu Dachi, Rei Dachi, Neko Ashi Dachi, Ippon Dachi, Hiza Dachi, Suwari Dachi, and Mae Suwari Dachi*) for at least one throw during the competition.
7. A panel of three judges scores the contestants for proper stance, technique, follow-thru and control after each round (scale .1 - 1.0). The scores are then averaged for each contestant and multiplied by the points scored for that round. (Example: If a contestant scored 60 points in a round and his average judges' score was .80, then his score for the round would be 60 × .80 or 48 points.)

SHURIKEN THROWING COMPETITION (INFORMAL)

The object of the competition is to be the first person or team to score 100 points.

Rules:

1. Each person may use the type of Shuriken of his/her choice.
2. Each person has 3 throws per turn, but is not required to throw all three during that turn. He/she may save them for the next round (see Strategy). However, he/she cannot accumulate more than 6 throws for any one turn. (Example: If you passed your turn at 8 feet and 10 feet, you would only get 6 throws at 15 feet, not 9 throws and you would, therefore, have lost 3 of the throws you passed on. Also, you could not use those 3 throws at 25 or 30 feet. They are lost.)

3. If your star knocks out an opponents star, that person would receive only half the points normally given. (See Strategy). All stars are removed at the end of each round.

4. To begin play, each person throws one star. Closest to the bull's eye starts, followed by the second closest, etc.

5. For following rounds, the first person up becomes the last up, the second up becomes first up, etc.

6. Contestants must use 5 of the 10 stances (*Kiba Dachi, Zenkutsu Dachi, Zenkutsu Dachi Gyaku Nage, Kokutsu Dachi, Rei Dachi, Neko Ashi Dachi, Ippon Dachi, Hiza Dachi, Suwari Dachi and Mae Suwari Dachi*) for at least one throw during the game.

Strategy

1. Throwing Order:
   Throwing first in the rotation has its advantages and disadvantages. The advantages include: being able to throw at a clean target without other stars cluttering the target area, even with a slight penetration your star will still score points (if its knocked off you still get ½ the point value.) The disadvantages include: all contestants who follow you have the opportunity to knock your stars off the target, being towards the end of the rotation gives you the option of throwing at a cluttered target (if previous contestants have thrown solidly planted scoring stars), or at a cluttered target (if previous contestants have thrown slightly penetrating scoring stars) with great potential to knock their stars off, or an uncluttered target (if previous contestants have not thrown stars which stuck).

2. Dislodging Stars:
   In regular competition and especially in formal competition, situations may arise where it is advantages to attempt to knock off another contestants stars which are in high point scoring areas of the target. That is, if they are close to winning or they have a large point advantage.

3. Stances:
   It is a good idea to use the more difficult required stances early in the game when the point values are lower, saving the easier stances for racking up high points.

Meditation Training

I have reserved this final section for the important aspect of mental training. Probably as important, if not more important than good technique and practice, mental training or meditation training is the key to heightened consistency and accuracy.

Not a religious training, my meditation training is utilized by martial artists to improve all aspects of their art by harnessing the elusive force often called *Ki, Chi* or a variety of other terms. Without going into a long explanation as to why *Ki* works or how it helps a person development, I will merely give you brief steps to develop it for your own uses.

Start by finding an isolated spot where noises and other distractions are at a minimum. Light a candle and place it on a small table approximately 3 feet high. With your back to the lit candle, assume the *Seiza* or seated position with legs together, knees bent under and back straight. (If this position is not comfortable for you, find a position that is comfortable.) Begin with 2 minutes of breathing in bursts. Inhale in short bursts, hold for a few seconds then exhale in short bursts. Continue in a uniformed pattern for the full 2 minutes.

During this exercise you should try to concentrate totally on balance and straightness, avoid tensing your muscles, making your body rigid.

Now, without getting up, slide around and face the lit candle. Concentrate on the candle flame only. Try to clear your mind of all distracting thoughts and feelings. Breathe smoothly, inhale, hold, exhale. Continue for 2 minutes or until the mind is clear and the body is relaxed.

Visualize a Shuriken in your hand. Examine it, grip it, feel it. Continue this process until the Shuriken image is sharp. In your mind, imagine that it is an extension of your arm. When you throw it at a target your arm is actually extending out across the distance and placing it in the target.

Mentally practice each throw, with proper technique, breathing and follow-thru. Remember that the star is not leaving your hand but your arm is extending out to place the star in the target.

Meditation training should precede each practice session.

Advanced Meditation Training

Briefly, advanced meditation training involves training to perfect and increase the awareness of the senses. With consistent practice the martial artists can take a mental photograph with his eyes, then close them and allow his other senses to move around and adjust that photograph. Example: the martial artist looks at a room, closes his eyes and walks around with ease, because he is constantly adjusting that mental photo by input from his other senses.

Training is focused on understanding and becoming aware of the smallest inputs from the various senses and allowing the subconscious mind to process and control the body.

This is also known as perception training or heightened sensitivity.